Want

Want

POEMS
Rick Barot

Sarabande Books

LOUISVILLE, KENTUCKY

FIRST EDITION

Managing Editor
Sarabande Books, Inc.
2234 Dundee Road, Suite 200
Louisville, KY 40205

Library of Congress Cataloging-in-Publication Data

Barot, Rick, 1969-
Want : poems / by Rick Barot. — 1st ed.
p.   cm.
ISBN 978-1-932511-57-4 (pbk. : acid-free paper)
I. Title.
PS3602.A835W36 2008
811'.6—dc22
2007010578

ISBN-13: 978-1-932511-57-4

Cover image: *Abandoned Apartment, near Rosenstrasse, Dresden.*
© 2005, Fredrik Marsh. Provided courtesy of the artist.

Cover and text design by Charles Casey Martin

Manufactured in Canada
This book is printed on acid-free paper.

Sarabande Books is a nonprofit literary organization.

THE KENTUCKY ARTS COUNCIL

The Kentucky Arts Council, a state agency in the
Commerce Cabinet, provides operational support funding for
Sarabande Books with state tax dollars and federal funding from
the National Endowment for the Arts,
which believes that a great nation deserves great art.

to Consorcia Alvarez Barot
and Maria Omega Pascua

CONTENTS

—//—

ACKNOWLEDGMENTS

—✻—

I am grateful to the editors of the following publications for
publishing the poems in this volume:

Agni Online ("Magnolia"); *Blackbird* ("Psalm with a Phrase
from Beckett"); *Black Warrior Review* ("Pescadero"); *The Canary*
("The Horses"); *Five Fingers Review* ("Captivity Narrative");
Gulf Coast ("After Heraclitus," "Cut Piece," "Say Goodbye,
Catullus, to the Shores of Asia Minor"); *New England Review*
("Echo," "K." "Like a Fire That Consumes All Before It"); *The
New Republic* ("Litany"); *Pleiades* ("West 16th Street"); *Poetry*
("Elegy"); *Post Road* ("Two Video Installations," "December");
The Seattle Review ("Theories of the Visible"); *Slate* ("Iowa");
Southwest Review ("Constitution Gardens," "Early Greek
Thinking," "Sonnet," "Washington Circle"); *TriQuarterly*
("Pastoral"); *The Yale Review* ("Fin Amor").

"Many Are Called" was printed in *Legitimate Dangers: American
Poets of the New Century* (Sarabande Books, 2006) and
reprinted in *Contemporary Voices of the Eastern World: An
Anthology of Poems* (W. W. Norton, 2008). "West 16th Street"
was reprinted in *Tigertail: A South Florida Annual* (Tigertail
Productions, 2006). "Elegy," "The Horses," and "West 16th
Street" were reprinted in *Under the Rock Umbrella:
Contemporary American Poets from 1951–1977* (Mercer
University Press, 2006). "The Horses" was reprinted on *Verse
Daily*. "Pastoral" was reprinted on *Poetry Daily*.

For gifts of time, space, and camaraderie, I'm happy to thank The George Washington University, Lynchburg College, the MacDowell Colony, and Pacific Lutheran University, particularly my colleagues in the English Department. My gratitude to the following, whose encouragement helped along the way: David Borrelli, Michael Dumanis, Monica Ferrell, Rigoberto Gonzalez, James Hoch, Benjamin Jackson, Alex Lemon, Jonathan Liebson, John Lincoln, Cate Marvin, David Roderick, Salvatore Scibona, Brian Teare, Brian Umana, C. Dale Young. I am grateful to Jason Luker, these poems' first listener.

I know what I have given you. I do not know what you have received.

—Antonio Porchia

Echo

And what part of his reflection will tell me who I am,
that I am standing a little away, wanting in on his story?

Days I am *cup, slice, gray, need, therapy*. The headache
of the repetition of his voice, telling himself some story.

I am in the city looking for him, forcibly drawn to
the square glass eyes. A light is on in the hundredth story.

Street black as an eel, the wavering look of him inside
its puddle. I play lamp-post to the dark of this story.

The one who sets fire to half the state while setting fire
to letters in the forest. Let her be part of this story.

I am myself in lace, rubber things, oil on every bit of
my body, whip-talk. He loves only the mirror's story.

A pistol, a knife, plastic tubing, plastic trash bags, spray
gun, a wig, a brick of cash. These are the start of a story.

The one who wrote the letters to begin with, his flawed
love like violets in her hand. Let him be in the story.

Later, the weasels and the otters coming to the stream
to pull up the roots, husked like onions. Eating his story.

Staring into his winter face, lips blue as Krishna because of his winter face. No one ever got this piece of the story.

I get to be the woods, quiet just under the tongue-tied lightning, the ever-responding thunder. Bleak with story.

Theories of the Visible

1.

Marble nipple that no tongue or fingertip
can make come alive: I love the deliberate
chiseling accorded even to the brailled
texture surrounding the stiff eraser-like tip,

one Greek's careful attention poured hand
and eye into the torso's unharmed white,
standing now for what was there, what must
have breathed and warmed just beyond

the sculptor's touch, the prerogative *no*
of the youth something I can only imagine,
no worked into the cold sinew, the utterly
soft cock. Like a Hermes on winged

2.

feet, the boy of one summer is rollerblading
naked in the house, all summer singing
with the stereo's rutting synthetic thumps,
the two neighbors glaring at our door

greeted by the boy who was wearing nothing.
Every night, one of us always left without

sleep, amphetamine-strung, opening
books, doors, and drawers whose cool air

was awake in their dark. I'd watch his eyes
in their sleep, crimped like a poppy's
petals, reeling from their own black seeds.
In the codes of passion the Florentines

3.

held during the Renaissance, it was nothing
for a man and his friends to raid another
man's house and take his wife, the deaths
acceptable enough a price for that one love.

In that city of architecture, of strict theories
of the visible, perspective made a science,
I love how emotion unraveled matter
into metaphor, the mouth a star, the elbow

a kingdom. Writing of his mistress's pale
beauty, Lorenzo de Medici likened it
to the delicate white fat condensed around
an animal's kidneys, as though seeing had

4.

to pierce that far, with its pen or its scalpel,
to know itself. That summer, we'd walk

to the nearby park and look at the acres being
restored back to prairie, their blaze of dried

grasses and reeds, the mice running out
from the edges, and then back. A mile away,
the baseball stadium at dusk would roar
with people and light, a spaceship landed

on the prairie's ghost expanse. I knew
to steal against what would be lost: the sugar
dispenser from a diner's table, his fingers'
taste of dirt, the bats separating from the tree,

5.

each a manic franchise of the gloaming black.
For the painters of Lorenzo's time, flesh
was a lie. Trusting an improbable alchemy,
first they applied a layer of green onto

the body on a canvas, then incremental layers
of red. In the end, the blossoming flesh
appeared there, lit from within like a pear.
In the oldest paintings, you can see the green

and blue in their cracked faces, the cold
origin just beneath. What little they needed
to make the miraculous: red clay, sulfur,
gold powder, egg yolk, mercury, marble dust,

6.

and salt, each thing ground down for another
purpose. It was a rented summer's house.
We were going to walk away from each other.
For a week he had a fever, and what I knew

was his sleep, a body and its breathing.
And already I understood the blue current
that would extend from where I was to where
I would be, ignited with that life. Days after

his fever, we saw a crow slowly take apart
a greasy paper bag on the grass, holding
down the bag with a foot as it ate each ripped
dirty piece. What is it to be here but to want?

Many Are Called

to burn at least one thing they once owned: she tears
the page from his book and sets light to whatever
she said to him there, words to smoke, paper

to black snow. She would like a sleep as big as
a building, whose key she firmly keeps in her hand,
its teeth writing into her palm. *Be as nothing*

in the floods, I read yesterday on the bus home,
which was a way of saying that in the dimmed glass
all of us and none of us could be found. But one

face was like sun reflecting on ice, lit by what
the Walkman poured into it, its champagnes. One
made me think of the mushroom in the woods

like a face pressed to a photocopier's flash,
the face and its goofy pain. Many are called to save
what they can: he rolls up his pants and wades

into the fountain, where the gull has its leg caught
on a wire. The bird flaps away to join the wheeling
others, their strokes on the air like diacritical

marks over the sentences uttered below them.
A friend writes about how cold he had been, nearly
drowned in the spring-melt river when the horse

tipped over. It is months away now, but still
I have him there, in the darkening field, the fireflies
a roused screensaver. Many are called to close

upon themselves like circles: Kafka, waking because
a dog is lying on him. He doesn't open his eyes
but he can feel its weight, its paw smelling

faintly of hay. Or the woman crying in the park,
her shopping cart tumbled, shoes and cans spilled out
like junk from a shark's stomach. Or the man

walking home along the houses and the lawns
of his sadness: *If there must be a god in the house* . . .
Under the new trees and the new moon of his sadness:

He must dwell quietly. Many are called to form
a deity out of what they know: he quizzes me
on the capital of every African country, he paints

his toenails silver because I ask him. A friend writes
about the church where a fresco will always show
them: cleanly naked at first, then full of the blame

of their own guile, then clothed, worried with age,
the woman in her room setting fire to something
she had, the man in the meadow, wishing his rib back.

Two Video Installations

The elephant in the white room
is told to play dead, and she falls

to the gray floor, rocking a little
before going completely still,

only to wake again, rocking again
a few times to find momentum

and push herself onto a splayed
position on the floor, her legs

spread like a skirt, and then
the methodical lifting of each leg

so that each gains its footing,
each lifting her a little until she is

fully up, wholly still once more
until some voice in the room

tells her to die again, all of her
wrinkled bulk made blank canvas,

wet stone for an eye, the camera
moving around her as though

she were the center of a carousel
around which the other animals

galloped and leapt up and brayed.
On another screen, one man's

rapture of grief is told in a face
gone blurry as paint sliding

down a wall, a woman's crying is
an open mouth black with depth,

a woman prays, her hands knotted
into white roots, while another

man standing behind the others
cannot decide whether a howl or

a laugh is what's needed in this
moment after they have been told

to think the worst thing they can
remember, the moment then slowed

to sixteen minutes of quiet film,
so that even the thoughtless blink

of an eye takes a few minutes
to satisfy itself, the pixels changing

like cells under a lens, the last
woman an opera of disbelief about

what has come to pass for them
in the dim room, her face a metal

of rage, the voice somewhere
demanding every form of sorrow

from them, and, having been asked,
this is how they had to answer.

Captivity Narrative

1.

He is running across the ice

fast enough so that it doesn't know it should

be breaking. At some point

you will breathe again. This could be

a movie, will be the movie you play

when you tell the story somewhere,

sometime, else: this boy in the avocado

windbreaker, the sky the white

of pills. In one of the captivity narratives

you have read, the Indians took a woman

on an ice floe big as a room.

You don't know anything yet.

You are on this side still. The ice

is scarred like the moon.

2.

If his eyes were brown, you should

have known this. You thought they were green.

If there is money in his pockets,

you should know this; think of licking

the hands clean. You can ask with some

pleasure, *Why do you smell like gym?*

You want the paradigm love

you think of all day

to become the tender machines of fact.

Something is like a spigot, another like a toaster.

His thumb flicks on the lighter,

hinges stop things from falling apart.

The planes keep going over cities, intricate below

as the insides of watches.

3.

The streets of your city are white.

But from where he is, he writes about the muezzin

calling the heat's changes—

heavier, then less. The blue

concentrated day, curved: he wears his headphones

walking in the gold market.

In other words he writes the insect-like script

for *lemon* and *electric*,

each a bladed, calligraphic secrecy.

Here, the plastic stapled over your windows

keeps the cold out. In a dream that you wake from,

the bug skitters

into your ear, rapid with fright, eating its way

to the other side.

4.

　　　Still, you are no more certain

for every image you have. His figure

　　　　　up ahead, the tree stripped, each

item warped into something you need.

The chair is peeling outside under a waterlogged

　　　sky. The child is asked,

Why is your face so dirty? You are no more happy

　　　　for having seen them:

　　　in the bus, a girl rubbing her nose

on the boy's cheek, the life of the streets fiercely

passing, moving. It is an industry, love.

　　　　The tree's fingers brightening

into your notice one day, the child holding

　　　a coin in his mouth.

5.

When he is five and his father

has not yet lost it, they would climb to

the top floor of the downtown

building and put mail into the old-fashioned chute

that fell all the way down, a glass

spine. You see the scrawled North Pole

address, the sepia-colored stamp showing

the Wright Brothers and their plane.

This many years later, just outside

the museum, he says he sees his father, skinny

as a string, dirty Santa beard, garbage clothes.

He would like to kick him

for what he did and didn't do. He would like to

take him with him.

6.

First they arranged a circle

of flat stones, then smaller rocks and a layer

of sand. Then twigs,

and bunched, dry grass, and larger pieces

of wood. The fire caught quickly where one

of the men had struck one, from out

of his hands. From that long captivity,

now back to a home of particular

rooms, what returned to her came

in a colorless stream, things recalling

only themselves. The curiously solid footing

of the ice, the fire

they made on it. And the snow, the sky coming

down to the ground.

7.

        You will have to keep traveling.
This far north the light will not sleep.

                So there must other ways of being
held. Can it be that there is only one bird,
only one: *Who made the eyes but I?*

        One barn and its stricken panes:
Where are my window songs? Backyard pools

             are blue as his envelopes,

       though the leaves have dropped, shadows
clumped at the bottoms. You're walking
not knowing you're walking, just someone

              turning in sleep, someone turning
a corner and appearing unannounced

           on a storefront's dozen TVs.

THE HORSES

The primary red striped onto the black, the dye
        spotting the mirror and sink with
a kind of gore, a sulfur that is in the air for days:
        you are twenty-two and this means

even folly has its own exacting nature. The hair
        turned red, as easily as last month's
blue; the puggish, miniature barbell pierced into
        a nipple. At the club I watch you on top

of the speaker, tearing the shirt your brother gave
        you, the music a murderous brightness
in the black room. Now you want it all off, down
        to clear scalp. Your head in foam,

you ask me to do the places you can't properly
        reach: the neck's mossy hairs, the back's
escarpment, an edge of bone the razor nicks
        to small blood, tasting like peppermint

and metal on my tongue. In the used-bookstore
        this afternoon, in the master's book of
drawings, pencil sketches of the heads of horses,
        whose long nostrils had been slit open

as custom demanded. The Icelanders, Mongols,
and Italians finding a measurable
efficiency in what they could see: the horses, even
in their speed, as though not breathing.

MAGNOLIA

A story gets told, begins to hold fast,
and like rain brings back a thing more

than just itself, one more small noise
appearing in the laundromat, small bird

or cell-phone ring suddenly chirping,
one more office for the eye and ear

to momentarily inhabit, the work of my
nearness that much more urgent, now

there is this story I can tell you about,
now I have you listening, the way

the radiator has kept us listening all of
these nights, the din of its dreaming

the noise of picks and axes deep inside
a mine, the steam in its pipes forcing

a drowsiness on the miners, listening
for some other dream it could have:

say, that two people are quiet within
the cold light of an all-night laundromat,

the only thing open this late, this dark,
one of them telling a story of the dead

president traveling days past the big
and small towns, his train a vivid grief

of flowers thrown by the townspeople
beside the tracks, one telling this

story while the other only half listens,
until the story gets to the part about

the summertime heat, the body traveling
for days, the flowers a necessary cover

for the smell the body is giving out,
there is this other way that flowers can

mean something, not just mourning, not
just beauty, but a necessity that keeps us

awake through the story, the radiator's
other dream, half of their clothes making

a psychedelic circle of colors spinning
in the glass of a dryer, the white clothes

spinning in another dryer, like a magnolia
opening and destroying itself over and

over, the image a nearness, my being
near, my being afraid that this is already

the past I will remember in the future,
this is the meat that the mind's mandibles

get to have, dying, because death gets
to have all it wants: say, the doctor's

funhouse reflection in the patent-leather
shoe of the dead president, the boy who

finally understands that the secret to
getting hit is knowing that you will be hit,

the flight attendant mis-speaking to us
as the plane glided toward the starry field

that we would be *in* the ground shortly,
and though I laughed at that, I knew

I would find the right word for you, place
it into her mouth, the flower of it in her

mouth, I would correct the world in this
manner, because you are listening, it is

raining outside the laundromat, the driest
part of your body the small of your back.

WEST 16TH STREET

Light glossing on the breakers, then disappearing.
You say it is mortal that way: silver, then gone.
On the phone, it becomes the distance I listen for,
the waves talking just behind you. Here, it is quietly
confusing to be at this height, the city's colors

rising to an electric sky, its dense gray yellowed,
drawing from neons, chimneys, and windows
which declare themselves awake, for now.
For clarity, I pick one car pulsing among the red
sequence on the bridge; I follow to where its road

ends, headlights staring into a wall of trees.
You tell me how you were in the ocean for hours,
the heaving that took you under for deep seconds,
the salt warmth flowing from your nose and ears
long after you left the water. Tonight, you are

as far away as that house suddenly lit behind
the trees, a pond taking in the light rain, the leaves
dropping into it. The traffic on the bridge lessens,
some windows go out for the night. Sleep
might be a water shuddered into, or a mere falling.

It is not lasting mercy. It is only brightness or
it is dark. I cannot stop the surf from taking you in,

or the leaves from dissolving to silt. You stand
by the shoreline on another coast, and to me this
may be the form of perfect wanting, the logic

of a heart unsatisfied. But it is not purpose, it is
not proof. The meadow in the dream is polite
at first. Then wind slams every window and door,
testing the soundness of an argument. I will wake.
Something will be finished, the morning will be sad.

Pastoral

Here is the dusk with a pink plastic bag
      in the tines of a branch, the wheeze

in the wind's throat before the wind lies
      down on the water. Here is the brink

revealing the icy spring's pulmonary
      green, the grasses softly becoming.

The water is like the darkest part of an x-ray
      sheet, possessing into itself

the shadows building between trees, shrubs
      roundly black like pots. Traced onto

nothing, here is my grandfather trying to
      push breath out of his locking lungs,

my memory dividing like the enraged cells:
      his papery, hollowed-out face;

the brown broth of herbs he sipped, trying
      to outwit what had lodged in him

for good. It's stupid to keep seeing the body
      in the world, its breath and song

wrongly illuminated in the salary of images:
        hospital tubes in a coiled garden

hose, the plastic bag in the tree waiting
        like a lyre. And yet by these errors

what's beneath is sometimes fathomable:
        you running on the Potomac's banks,

your lungs pumped with the medicine that
        cures you as it didn't my grandfather,

the rain drumming mist out of the ground,
        the mud a gradually clinging weight.

Heading back, you decide to scale a country
        club's wall, diving naked into

the unguarded pool to wash off the mud.
        You tell me this as I try to unfurl your

hands, and you finally open them, showing
        damage that a door or hammer has

brought on each knuckle, the outlasting scars
        coarse as the nodes on a branch.

Early Greek Thinking

1.

Even they understood
that the ideal is a fantasy.

2.

Pummeled by the justice
of time, the ideal is broken

like the cracked vase in
the museum, on which have

been painted naked hoplites
carrying shields, riding

cherubic dolphins.

3.

Later, in Petrarch, an old

man leaves his village,
like a patient lover finally

needing the violence of
an answer, and journeys to

the holy city to see the true
and graven face, having

only seen the image, brief
watermark, on a miracle

tree trunk, on the strangely
spotted fur of a housecat.

4.

This morning, still sleeping,
your face seemed sweet,

a coin under water. It was
as though you weren't there.

5.

There was peace in the house.

PESCADERO

Because half the fog is in, the brunt of it
        still out in the middle ground of graying
water, this curved cell of the coastline

resolves to be its particulars in the flatly drained
        light. Tide out, caves freed
of water, the rocks are like the scarred humps

of something that will not wake. We are a *we*
        only because no one is here,
scrambling down the damp, orange dirt

of the slope, to the cove without motion or wind.
        The nearer shore is made
of egg-smooth stones in gray and white corian

shades; further on, just at the water, the scab
        rocks that should be underwater.
Would be underwater: starfish in the tide-pools,

cockles purple as eggplants, and anemones with
        crimped centers which close
at the brush of a finger. These are things

I have to be told about. Otherwise there is only
             the mess of what I don't know
to look for. "Eel grass," he says, from his sharper

version of what's here. The grass is hard green
             in color, sturdier than you'd think
for something always wet. Then the currents,

the waves he tells me about, our coast half in fog,
             half in leftover light, the air
cleanly refrigerated like a fish-store's. Because

it's spring, festering thick on the sand and rocks
             are the blue-silver bodies of
hydroids, shiny things even the gulls won't eat.

The size of silver dollars, heavy as an oil slick
             onshore, the creatures are another
thing he makes me see. And my version of things:

it's still caught on the highway we drove on
             to get here, a story of what his father did
drunk, nothing particularly good or bad,

just a childhood blurred into something like
             indifference now. And I know that what
I remember of all this will be far smaller

than the subtractions before us. How each atom
           within every stone moves always.
How a wave wears everything away. A wind goes

up and I say, "Let it be, motherfucker, let it be."
           In parts, the sun newly breaks in,
the fog thins. The light keeps changing, changing

what it touches, the gray water going gold at first,
           then green as an eye. I turn from
what I know is there, that true, concluding figure.

K.

Now I am the least sorry thing in the room.
The dark huddling like trees against the walls,

the cold. The one candle is an affectation,
its almond-shaped tip flaring; the frost arrives

on the windows. I leave behind the white
noise of other rooms, cities, the books whose

inks pool to my lap when I am not careful.
Pale as a petal, I ask that the rope be put on

tighter, so that the bones of my ankles knock
into each other. My wrists kiss. I understand

the greed of the actress, her vanity made
important: how the rouge of some emotion

gets slowly placed on the cheek of nothing.
And I understand the martyr's accepted

brokenness: no deliberation in the self now,
no more purpose left in his hands. Only

the pebbles pushing into his soles as he walks
on the path, the plinth of wood he is lifted

onto, the frank dryness of the sky. His head
tilts upward when the arrow breaks into

his thigh. Then the explosion on his cheek,
teeth crushed. And the deer in its shadow,

the deer in the cover away from the soldiers,
its mouth eating even the bark, even thorns.

LITANY

When any word is called for, say that I am *of*.
When the tornado forms, that is the ruinous
kiss. When the bamboo-green field sways,
think of tea. When the vines thicken in
the heat, this is the medusa head consuming
its own stare. When a man commitedly
steps to the ledge, this is the daguerreotype's
cold glass face. When winter, that is *hemlock*
prominent. When mirror or letter or echo,
these are correspondences. When the snow
is pink, something has been left motherless.
When singing, think of articulating silences.
When stars, history. When the sword-gray,
fatherly rain, this is *I have wandered the earth*.

Say Goodbye, Catullus, to the Shores
of Asia Minor

In the love as they know it, they take turns on their knees
at the altar that's never without one of them there, a prayer
unceasing in the chapel's small air. Midnight, the middle

of the night, then dawn, heat, the hills beyond the convent
turning deep green: the prayer continues unbroken for years,
one nun arriving to summon back to daylight the one

who has been praying all night, her voice a rosary bead
meant to be the exact circumference of the others, perfect
with belief. Meanwhile, a man faces one painting for twenty

years, only to find the question he had asked at the start:
What is in your sight now? On the canvas, the journey tells
a pilgrim's progress of paint scumbles, crayola scratches,

histories and jokes told, forgotten, found again, until the torn
head singing in the stream is the world singing: *his mortal
heart pressed out an inexhaustible wine.* In the book that

Brian lends me, he has penciled in things meant for no one
else to see: *dancing in forest, expressing self to you, breaking
up,* directives in the margins like papyrus bits coming

to us half-speaking, so that all day I walk around as though
a bowl were balanced on my head, the fish inside kissing
their glass perimeter. The convent is miles outside the city

where my grandmother spent the war making herself ugly:
soot on her face, rags to wear, her eyes on the street,
the newsprint blackness hiding her from what the Japanese

soldiers would have seen: *sampaguita, paddy, blood river*.
And what's underneath keeps rising to the crumb-specked
surface: John, jumping off the plane, jams into the door's

side, dislocates a shoulder, and tries to push it back in before
he passes out, falling, numbers in his head counting the time
when he has to pull the parachute. Outside, it is summer:

the clearing's downed birches are melting into rot, chip
by chip. From this distance they seem a painter's sketch of
drapery, the sheets covering something passed away,

machine or horse's rib-cage or an old man sleeping, blind,
wisdom at one entrance quite shut out, the ants investigating
the folds, the sockets, the nose-holes. Streets, houses,

remnant names murmured late in a meal: my grandmother
tells us who collaborated, how they cheered in the hills
when the planes finally arrived, whose babies were thrown

toward the bayonets. Told now as if an afterthought: all
that was cunningly lived through and seen from this
soft shore. Finishing his painting, the painter draws a boat

already fading into the water, its black shape exhausted
by the white water, and the old poet is so silent with grieving
that he has to be given the word of his farewell. Tell each

story cold, I tell myself. Tell it dark: the berry eyes of deer
among trees. Tell it without need of an answer: a man falls
from a plane, my grandmother washes her face, the boat

survives. Outside, it is summer: the spore's ground zero,
the thistle's battlements, the hypercium's red and phallic buds,
the chinaberries in the thickets small as vowels, the white

veins in the translucent red. The berries in the glass: these
are what I will bring back, standing beneath the sparks
thrown by a trolley's hissing wires, the fire of a beginning.

Seven Poems

1. Constitution Gardens

The swallows' time. Not like fish schooling
into one contour of grace, but like leaves
scattering in a parking lot. The sun is gone,
just a little of it coating a plane's belly
orange. If I go down one street there is
the equestrian statue. Down another the milky
brown river. The day has these tributary
pools of mind. Go closer. It's like a new face
there. It is possible to have a life breathing
in this other way. It will not break or bruise,
nor be cause for pity or be site of elegy—
the lily below anyone's gaze, opened
white, blade leaves around it, a blaze of no
one's need but its own, burning underwater.

2. East

What took me so long to come back here?
Ghost limbs are ghosts for being lost.
But now this return, so that the bone
gets married to its other edge, the fibers
and fat piecing back together. If I lived

with the troubled air of what had gone
missing, I know the cost of my flamboyant
imagining. By my attention the tired
hospital seemed to go down, the wrecking
ball round and avid as an eye. Think
of sight breaking down tiled walls, stairs
and floors. Think of the pieces brought out
to yielding ocean. The windows were pried
out beforehand. The rubble didn't shine.

3. Washington Circle

I tell you how much it means for him to turn
around. She is still standing there, waiting,
though he has crossed the street, walked
a way down the sidewalk, only to finally stop
and wave. We talk about the precedent
for this, and the certain consequences, who
gets turned to stone. A sprinkler pays out
its lines of water, a man bathes at the park's
drinking fountain. What can I hope against all
your ocean? It is twelve hours later where
you are, the dawn unsullied, having hidden
its malfeasances in the dark. Through static
you say the houses glimmer in the outskirt
hillsides, like cinders. They are beautiful to see.

4. Fin Amor

Good is full of enterprise and evil is full
of enterprise, each thing a posited intention.
Country music is full of enterprise, salt
is, and saws are, and the stone is. Every metal
thing shines like a knight. Partial sun,
the clouds coaxed towards the bay because
of a hurricane thousands of miles away.
Your words are not happy, like afternoon
people on a train. I don't know what to send
back. If it is only two men walking small
dogs, one saying to the other: *They were bred
at first to be hors d'oeuvres*. If it is only
what's heard walking by a kitchen window:
You should see how bitter your mouth looks.

5. December

A white house in winter only loves its people
at night, dreaming. Otherwise, day is a murder
of glare: my tongue worries a seed lodged
between teeth, you build a tiny boat out of cedar.
Our sadness happens in real time; we might
as well be in Bergman. The white is that
white. A balloon is swallowed wholly by sky.
For a moment it was the day's only color:
the firefly-green of its disappearing. Quiet city:

44

the cold of politics is outside, an old man
with a cigarette between his fingers, a leaning
length of ash. He is writing the love poems
of his time, his pencil wounding the pages.
Quiet city: even the statues' eyes don't move.

6. After Heraclitus

The brushfire in the hills covets the town.
I laugh at the others, packing like Noah against
the slow, lion-gold paw of it. What is it
that needs saving? One neighbor's thousand
kewpie dolls, boxed in her car. Another one's
turtles, dim in a mossy terrarium. The papers
stuffed into shopping bags. The arrowheads in
a blue tobacco tin. Each letter that you sent me.
I imagine your call, coming when I'm finally
held to the corner, drinking the toilet's porcelain
water. I imagine your concern, useless after
the miracle of it, the wind pushing away the fire,
the blaze whispering disappointment: *Things
keep their secrets. Things keep their secrets.*

7. Sonnet

When moving from one house to another,
carry each container of sugar and rice and salt

into the house first. There will be gods happier
for this. My grandmother gives out such wisdoms,
the cerulean clarities of a faith. Or her other
lessons, unpleasant and tangled as the backs
of embroideries. Every morning you have mint
tea and translate words, prying them like diamonds
from a necklace, in the language of your own
grandmother. You watch the man pound
charcoal into ink. Then he prints the Arabic
onto a clean wooden tablet. Finished, he washes
the surface with water, catching the water into
a bowl, and drinks from the bowl and its ink.

Cut Piece

scissors to cuff, cutting

                around a line of wrist

scissors to collar, a hank

                of white fabric, white of neck

someone is taking one

                sleeve, cold seam where

the cutting is done

                one is starting on the hems

of pants, blue denim hoops

                small pliers to the stud

in the left lobe

                pliers to the exposed ring

in a navel, though careful

                they are like children

building a nest

                only it is a body

they are taking apart

                scissors up the length of leg

scissors up another

                pocket over the heart

coming undone

shirt white as breath coming

away in rough squares

body as bodhisattva

in the middle of the stage

pliably sleeping

through the belt's

unbuckling, hair being shorn

mouth opened to pry

the tongue-metal

like a rule of losing

brought to a clear system

the eyebrows are being

erased, the hair in the pits

the crossed legs unbent

for the blade

the fur on the arms

swept white, wiped infant

it takes this many hands

to make him disappear

what was taken away

now piled beside what is left

Psalm with a Phrase from Beckett

The boulder that is bigger than a house,
perched on the edge of another boulder, painted gold
and prayed to by monks in saffron robes.
This is you being somewhere for once.

The circle of men in the flea-market parking lot
pounding on paint buckets, conga drums, the noise bulky
and hot as a furnace. Tell them
they are heard!
                         If you are every morning
the world has ever had, the rose is the pharmacy
and brothel, visited and visited.
If I try to sing, it is like standing too long by the magazine
rack, a crime beheld by the clerk's warring eye.
Because that is your gazing too.

In one narrative of desire, the young poet can't see a field
for the field of broken stars
that has landed there among his own
and a lover's body.
                         Let the dark be longer for this.
Certain papers are made of rice hulls, lambs-wool, hemp
and bark, all the good bodies of things.
In that way of careful ingenuity, let everything
be made and broken and made again.

Walking home, I clink my knuckle against fences
and trunks, the moon coming up
behind the hills like a thought. By these means
at hand you can be proven.

                     Let the river clear of filth.
Let the young poet write his twenty-one poems,
one for every year of his age.

In still one more narrative about desire, a man makes
bracelets of the little bones of his neighbors,
selling them at the church fair. Let this be time
for you to drink the blue sludge
of airplanes.

            Tell me you are there.
Certain towns in the Midwest have radio towers as tall
as lighthouses, belated of a first ocean,
red eyes on their bodies like gods. Let the dark be longer
for this.

           Let the offered living hand
be an oar. There are armies the color of sand and of oil.
There are words exploding just under
the ground, too small for the dog to hear: *quaquaquaqua*.

Because that is your singing too.

ELEGY

In this rain we are moved to anecdotes.
That people float candles out to the river.
That in a field there is the crickets' grief.
It could be colder just now but it isn't.
Though there are the posters' missing faces.
Though a car is upside down, wheel turning.
The day will only want to keep arriving.
We will startle for the clothes by the bed.
For the vein glowing green on the thigh.
The coffee will come black inside its cup.
The bread will be made of something clean.
This will not seem enough and it isn't:
The white nouns of the moon, the paper.
The handkerchief pulled from an empty fist.

Like a Fire that Consumes All Before It

1.

You could say rain was in love with the world.
It poured on the mountains; the ocean lifted
to meet it. The woman was in her downtown
office, she was sure her children would at least
know to go to the roof, to wait there. Everything
was over a week or two later, though bodies
were still being found even in unexpected places.
In trees and wells, on shores on other islands.
The workers knew to look for the blue flame
glowing from the dirt, under which bodies lay.

2.

The woman at the dinner table carefully told us
there was a clamor when forklifts had to be used
to move the bodies. They were piled in the square,
having been collected from the shorelines, rivers,
from streets in town where the water and sludge
had carried them. There were too many of them
to be handled singly, and too few of the workers
to move them. After the bodies were put in trucks,
they were brought to the huge holes dug beyond
town. The ground was soft; the digging was easy.

3.

The workers didn't go home because their wives
couldn't stand the smell they brought with them.
When they could sleep, they remembered
their dreams. Instead they stayed up and smoked,
talking. If there were still trees, the mountain
would not have slipped away. To do the work,
they put on layers of rubber gloves. The bodies
were slick as fish, heavy as tires. They were past
having faces to study. If the workers were not
careful, the limbs would fall off from the weight.

4.

In his letter to her, the exclamation: *But for love!*
Can I help it? You are always new. Two hundred
years later, even the unexpectedly messy heath
was exuberant to us. Dogs crashed under shrubs,
a swan circled the dull pond, the massing of bent
trees held up the lowering sky, trying to rain.
He had seen all of this. At the house where
he was last fully alive, tourists walked on gravel
paths. In one room, a storytelling hour for children,
the man's voice a rising and falling boat at sea.

5.

Upstairs, among the hallways and rooms and fake
beds, his photocopied letters pinned to the walls.
Only here and there the beginning of a kind of
truth: her scrapbook of the day's fashions, lockets
of curled hair, the blood-drop gem on the ring
he gave her, the plum tree outside, its imagined
thrush. I thought of the small blue room he had
died in. Then the spot of currant jelly on the page
of a book, purple and blue, a color almost black,
the word for it he made in his letter to her: *purplue*.

6.

Going back to the Underground, we stopped by
a bookshop so crammed that we might have been
in the stomach or lungs of something barely
breathing. You looked at a print the woman said
was antique, its paper yellowed as though soaked
in tea: the back of a man, skin peeled to show
engraved muscles and veins. Too expensive,
I said, though she showed us the old date to prove
its age, lowering the price as we turned away,
bargaining as she had to, if we were going to stay.

7.

Certain small ferns, roadside goldenrod, spotted
tiger lilies. In particular the silver light the moon
applies, the road and field an ambrotype framed
in black velvet. The grasses have a collar's rubbed
silver shine. The fall is *grievy, brisk*. You want
to make a case for this, this ministering, the wick
of sight and your share of these things: *to desire
the honoure of the field*. How the meadow is
its layers of flowers, kinds of soils and kinds of
grasses, the broken bottles sugared on your lit path.

8.

The lupines are blue or yellow, or some mixed
blue and yellow, like speckled eggs. The birds
rise just ahead of the tractor's approach, the cows
are dumbly quiet. The awl of an ice-age advance
must have put the gully there. For three days
the moon has been as thin as a quill. In the fence
the nails bleed. There are stars and comets
on the rocks. The land is a silk green. A brailled
globe, spinning with a breath, a light touching
finger, a light finger, a touching finger, a finger.

9.

The sky has all these beginnings. The birds hover
over the water and feed. With light the ocean
assumes its adjectives. The chandelier rigging
of a spider's web is heavy with dew on a tree.
You are in the salamander's sublunary cool, eyes
emptying out of all their grief. There is never
an answer here. Only that you have to need
the justice of looking, even after everything else
you've seen. The bee by its touching recognizes
the blossom, like the blind man's hands on a face.

10.

The August of his dying. The hospital bed now
in the dining room, the machines alive: pump
and ventilator, even the small fan turning its face
to him over and over, quizzically. The tubes ran
red and then clear. All day the house was dark
as a theater, as though none of us could know
the outside: the daughters in the kitchen making
bitter cures, grandchildren made to inhabit books.
So many pills, a clipboard had to account for
each swallowed. The bed was becoming a door.

11.

His face was no longer one. Ocean in his lungs,
the pancreas a blackened coral. The least noise
scraped into a thistle in his ear, his breaths steep
with anger. In Dante there is that crowded ledge
where the shades eat themselves over and over,
the sockets of their draining eyes now like rings
with the gems pried out. The O of one eye, the M
of the empty nose, the O of the other eye spelled
the body's new name. Dante wondered, how could
an apple's smell, or a spring, lead to this hunger?

12.

When you are young you live within your eyes,
when you are old you live in your mind. But even
in his old age he lived in the world: his trousers
always ironed, shirts crisply stiff as paper, shoes
shined to light, in his pocket a wad of money
held by a rubber band. His anger had a kingliness,
vain and sad. Before dying he made sure that
everyone was there, the subjects of his posturing
and his love. My mother flew across the country;
he died when he heard her car door slam outside.

13.

In the story of Echo, I love that moment when
it becomes clear that nothing of what she says
will move him. Every word is a shipwreck, every
word a fury of his turning away. There is no
transformation left for her, except death. He sees
only himself, and in that there is also a death.
She can say all she wants to whom she desires—
nothing of it will be accepted by his hearing,
as he bends there, gazing at water, or aiming at
the auburn deer, his gestures an offhand cosmos.

14.

It is as the scholar in his lecture suggests—how,
in the moment of Echo's speaking, of her eager
response, she is most fulfilled but also most effaced,
because she is not speaking her own word, only
aping back what is not hers. At the library I looked
into *fire* and thought that etymology is also a kind
of biography. *Fier is known to be fier by the heat*
is one good beginning for her story. *I shall sett*
all his londes in fyre is one ending. The klaxon
consonants, the moon-like vowels eclipsing earths.

15.

She is invisible until she is dead. And then her
image is revealed at last, something dreamed about,
something of art, valuable because it is loved
by strangers. At the library I thought of her, how
the tenacious heart doesn't end, though no illusion
has held up, no premise or structure still stands.
At the next table, a homeless man slept, a fly
circling above the black nest of his hair, above
the sooty heap of his things, circling like the voice
she let go of, just to see what would come back.

16.

We were kids together in Europe, tracking bands.
He loved Russian novels, and when he spotted
the samovar in a London flea-market, he bought it.
We traded putting it into his backpack and then
in mine, the weight of it gaining as the two months
went by. Its body was a tall cool silver shape;
it had three short legs shaped like a lion's paws.
In it we kept money and weed. I would wake up
missing him, though he was always there: cigarette
cough, freckle, white fang, every sonnet's flower.

17.

He made me see cities. We would be on the bridge
and also talk about the bridge. It was sweet to be
part of a city's amnesia. The rain would do that
to us. Then each skyline would glow like a crown.
The green hearts of summer leaves on the trees,
and in that activity of the world was my fresh,
ticker-tape sight. There are the things the body will
take into itself, things harbored and lost at once,
like water changed from ice to liquid to lost air.
He was lost into my mind. The story began there.

18.

Some years later I was in his apartment, years since
I had seen him last. The samovar was on a low
table. One girlfriend or another had turned it into
a vase out of which peacock feathers bloomed, blues
and greens iridescent, yellow impenetrable eyes.
I didn't know him anymore, but the samovar was
still there, a reminder to the eye to correct the heart.
If I believed in love's necessary mutability, I had
also come to believe in what could be kept, the silver
bearing the ashes of all my living and all my dead.

Iowa

It is something to be thus saved,
         a point on which the landscape
comes to a deep rest.

The ore of a death held
         frozen, there in the gull so far
inland, embedded in the ice

at the river's edge. Its bulk
         in the thick gloss is darker
than the ice, shoe-shaped,

only the spoon-curved head
         telling you what it is, one eye
open though no longer seeing.

The feet are ribbed, like sails
         tight on a mast. And a thing,
you remember, obliges by lying

down, its back to sky. How long
         it has been like this, this little
a question to the world.

How small of a happening, though
      it happened because
there is witness of it. The width

of water utterly silent,
      the distance a pencil-smudge
of Chinese hills. First its fall,

then immersion, every air discovered
      out of each quill,
its feathers matted with grit.

The day is a white octave, breathing
      its snow, and the bird
delicate, like a bone inside the ear.

NOTES

—*//*—

"Two Video Installations": Douglas Gordon, "Play Dead: Real Time" (2002) and Bill Viola, "The Quintet of Remembrance" (2000).

"Many Are Called": The first italicized lines are from William James; the two lines subsequently italicized are from Wallace Stevens's "More and More Human, Oh Savage Spirit."

"Captivity Narrative": The final section quotes two lines from poems by George Herbert, the first italicized quotation from "Love (III)," the second from "Dullness."

"The Horses": The artist invoked in the final part of the poem is Pisanello.

"West 16th Street": The final line paraphrases Antonio Porchia, translated by W.S. Merwin: "When everything is finished, the morning is sad." The collection's epigraph, by Porchia, is also translated by Merwin.

"Early Greek Thinking": The reference is to Petrarch's sonnet 16 in *Canzoniere*.

"Pescadero": The hydroids, or jellyfish, are "Velella velella," also known as "By-the-wind Sailor."

"K.": A single-line entry from Kafka's *Diaries*: "I am supposed to pose in the nude for the artist Ascher, as a model for a St. Sebastian."

"Say Goodbye, Catullus, to the Shores of Asia Minor": The title is from Cy Twombly's monumental painting of the same name in the Menil Collection in Houston. The italicized line in the fifth stanza is one of Twombly's scrawls on the painting. In the 12th stanza, the line quoted is from Milton's *Paradise Lost*.

"Seven Poems": The final italicized sentences in "After Heraclitus" are from Heraclitus, in the translation by Brooks Haxton.

"Cut Piece": After Yoko Ono's 1964 performance piece, "Cut Piece."

"Psalm with a Phrase from Beckett": The italicized phrase in the penultimate line is from Lucky's speech in Samuel Beckett's *Waiting for Godot*.

"Like a Fire That Consumes All Before It": The title is from a panel in Cy Twombly's 10-painting series, "Fifty Days at Iliam," in the Philadelphia Museum of Art. The poem's first three sections are about the flood of 1992 in Ormoc City, the Philippines, in which 8,000 people were killed. In section four, the lines italicized are from a letter by Keats. The incident recounted in section 11 is from the *Purgatorio*, Canto 23. In section 15, the italicized sentences are from the *OED*.

In section 18, line seven paraphrases a line engraved on the William Hogarth memorial in London: "And through the Eye correct the Heart."

Photo by David Borrelli

THE AUTHOR

—⸎—

Rick Barot was born in the Philippines and grew up in the San Francisco Bay Area. His first book, *The Darker Fall*, was the winner of the Kathryn A. Morton Prize in Poetry and was published by Sarabande Books in 2002. His poems and essays have appeared in numerous publications, including *The New England Review, The New Republic, Poetry*, and *The Virginia Quarterly Review*. His work has also appeared in many anthologies, including *The New Young American Poets, Asian American Poetry: The Next Generation*, and *Legitimate Dangers*. In 2001 he received a poetry fellowship from the National Endowment for the Arts. He has taught at Stanford University, California College of the Arts, The George Washington University, and Lynchburg College. He lives in Tacoma, Washington, and teaches both in the Program for Writers at Warren Wilson College and at Pacific Lutheran University.